Dream
Dream interpretation

The complete guide to understanding dreams

New and Updated – 2nd Edition

By Angel E. Love

© 2016 – All rights reserved

© Copyright 2016 - All rights reserved.

In no way is it legal to reproduce, duplicate, or transmit any part of this document in either electronic means or in printed format. Recording of this publication is strictly prohibited and any storage of this document is not allowed unless with written permission from the publisher. All rights reserved.

The information provided herein is stated to be truthful and consistent, in that any liability, in terms of inattention or otherwise, by any usage or abuse of any policies, processes, or directions contained within is the solitary and utter responsibility of the recipient reader. Under no circumstances will any legal responsibility or blame be held against the publisher for any reparation, damages, or monetary loss due to the information herein, either directly or indirectly. Respective authors own all copyrights not held by the publisher.

Legal Notice:

This book is copyright protected. This is only for personal use. You cannot amend, distribute, sell, use, quote or paraphrase any part or the content within this book without the consent of the author or copyright owner. Legal action will be pursued if this is breached.

Disclaimer Notice:

Please note the information contained within this document is for educational and entertainment purposes only. Every attempt has been made to provide accurate, up to date and reliable complete information. No warranties of any kind are expressed or implied. Readers acknowledge that the author is not engaging in the rendering of legal, financial, medical or professional advice.

By reading this document, the reader agrees that under no circumstances are we responsible for any losses, direct or indirect, which are incurred as a result of the use of information contained within this document, including, but not limited to, —errors, omissions, or inaccuracies.

Table of Contents

Introduction

Why Lucid Dreams Happen

A Little on Why You Dream

How to Enhance Your Lucid Dreams

Why You Want to Remember Dreams

Starting to Analyze Your Dreams

Understanding Preparation Essentials

Some Dream Methods

A Little on Nightmares

Some Common Meanings

Dreams & Meditation

Dreams & Positive Affirmation

Mindfulness & Your Dreams

Dream Tips & Reminders

A Guide to Settling in to Dream

Some More Dream Symbols

Some Dream Trivia

Conclusion

Introduction

In this book you'll learn everything that you'd want to know about dreams, including why we have them. When people dream, there is usually a deeper reason, and there's a meaning that you can derive from them if you know what to look for.

The main reason for this book is to shed some light on the topic of dreams and even open your mind to lucid dreaming. This book covers why lucid dreaming happens, what your dreams could mean, and even teach you about different dreaming methods. You'll learn about sleep continuity, sleep interruption and even reality checks in this dream, helping you to induce lucid dreaming and the concepts that it entails.

Before we begin, here is a small GIFT for you. It is from my publisher as a thank you for buying this book.

The Ultimate Beginners Guide to Yoga – Get it FREE!

What is Yoga?

Why is Yoga beneficial?

What are the different kinds of Yoga?

What are the different types of Yoga Equipment and Accessories?

Get answers to all your above questions in this FABULOUS book. Reap amazing health benefits.

Please go to the below link and download for free

https://shininguniverseenergy.leadpages.co/beginners-guide-to-yoga/

Hope you like your gift.

And now let's get on with our topic of the day.

Why Lucid Dreams Happen

If you've experienced lucid dreams or want to learn about them, then this chapter will help you to learn about this phenomenon. This chapter will cover what lucid dreams are, why people experience them, and how you can experience them on person. Lucid dreams are dreams in which you become aware that you're dreaming. It's where your conscious connects to the dream you're having, allowing you to do things in the dream.

Many people will use lucid dreaming to fulfill fantasies, explore the dream world that your mind has created, and to just help to relieve stress. Lucid dreaming allows you to explore your dream with perfect clarity, allowing you to experience the dream as you would in true reality. It'll allow you to see people again, touch different objects, taste and smell new things. Your dream world is a virtual world, but it'll allow you to experience it as if it were real, allowing you to live out any fantasy that you desire.

Going More In Depth on Lucid Dreaming:

In this world, you're in complete control. If you want to time travel, shape shift, see exotic spices, become the hero, or anything else, you can do it. You can learn to fly, fight, or choose where your dream takes you. Many people will cover psychological issues in their dreams because their dreams are a safe environment for them to face their fears. If you can become lucid while in your safe space, you can face the phobias and fears that are harder to face in real life, helping you to overcome your own anxieties.

You can face the person that scares you, overcome an obstacle, or experience something that you've always wanted to. You can relieve past traumas to help you get over them. With lucid dreaming, you're in control of the outcome, so you can change the outcome of an event that was traumatizing, helping to change your mindset. This can help people to be more at ease and move on with their lives after horrible events or even in bad circumstances.

If you're creative, it's a great way to tap into that creativity as well, helping you to write books, practice art, and even make music. Even if you don't have a talent in the real world, you can see your imagination come to life in your dreams, helping you to get trapped ideas out to experience them. You can only seek these ideas out when you become lucid. Many famous artisans claim that their inspiration was from their dreams, such as Mary Shelley, who claimed that "Frankenstein" came from an extremely lucid and vivid nightmare. Albert Einstein even claimed that "The Speed of Light" was written after a vivid lucid dream as well.

What to Do When You Start a Lucid Dream:

Now that you know what a lucid dream is, you need to understand that these are visually rich and detailed dreams. Once one is started, you'll have a 360-degree view, allowing you to completely view the world that your mind has created around you. There are even other people that have claimed that in their lucid dreams they were able to create representations of other dimensions.

The land in your dreams is infinite because you can create it. There are no limits, boundaries or laws that you will need to abide by, so you can literally do anything that you want. Your will, will manifest around you, creating the world as you see fit. You can even become aware of the 'inner self' that you have, learning more about yourself than you've ever gotten the opportunity to know before. You can explore other universes as well, discovering new worlds, lands, manipulating matter around you, but you have to get to that point first. Don't worry, you'll get there.

Controlling Your Dreams:

Now that you know how amazing having a lucid dream is, your first question will probably be how to accomplish it. There are a few different ways you can reach this level of control in your dreams. The first thing you'll have to do is to become conscious in the dream environment. This will help you to shape your dream as you go through it. The first step is to say the desire out loud. If you want to create a butterfly, say "I want a butterfly right there." if you're lucid enough, you should be able to put power behind your words. The dream will create what you want if you are actually lucid.

Sometimes, a verbal command won't actually work, though. If for some reason a command doesn't work, then try to just 'will' it into existence. Make it an expectation, and concentrate on that expectation. If this doesn't work, then you aren't lucid enough yet. However, there are still a few more things that you can try, and keep in mind that practice really does make a difference. It isn't common to be able to take control of your dreams the first few times you try it, and so you need to enjoy the awareness that you have even if you aren't lucid yet. Try to be patient, and enjoy the vivid detail that you'll be able to remember.

A Little about Staying Lucid:

Even if you can become lucid in your dreams, it can be difficult to remain in control as well. Your dreams may even end prematurely. Sometimes it's due to the adrenaline rush that you experience, and this adrenaline will cause you to wake up before the dream is over. There's no reason to worry, as this is normal. Others will even forget that they were dreaming afterwards because the brain actually functions differently when asleep, making it easy to forget things the moment you wake up.

If you're trying to make your dreams go on longer, then you can try to keep your mind both focused and calm. Just remind yourself that you're dreaming, helping you to stay mentally grounded, and keeping you in your dream world a little longer. Rub your hands together, and state that 'I'm dreaming', which will help you to stay grounded. This sends a kinetic sensation to your brain, drawing awareness to your body in the dream, keeping actually away from reality. These are common techniques to keep you grounded in your dream.

Manipulating These Dreams:

Manipulating your dreams would be the next step, and you may not have an idea what to do just because the possibilities are endless. It's usually best to start small, and meeting a person that you want to or changing your scenery is considered to be an easier task than willing objects into the world. Mental block is one of the main complains that people have when they try to practice lucid dreaming because being a lucid dreamer requires you to focus your mind and have confidence.

Trying to find a 'dream door' is usually the best way to start, and it can be there no matter the landscape. You locate the object, and you then step through it. This will help you to go to another part of the world that you've created. However, this concept doesn't work for everyone, so you might want to make a mirror portal. A mirror portal is considered to be a mirror made of some kind of liquid that leads to another dimension, allowing you to choose your next environment because what you're stepping through can then be classified as 'magical', helping you to keep from being grounded by physics.

There are tons of creative solutions to help you control your dream, but the most important thing to remember is that you're conscious will shape this land. You just have to stay confident and believe in your ability, enjoying it but staying calm. You can do anything you want, but you have to stay completely focused. You can even make dream characters which are completely different people or they can be people that you know. To do this, you need to heighten your lucidity and attempt to visual the person that you're hoping to meet. It can be someone new, another version of yourself, or someone that you know.

A Little on Why You Dream

Most people don't even know why we dream. You may be wondering if it's something that your brain just biologically does, if there is a physiological reason, or if it's just a psychological function. The question of why we dream hasn't been answered yet, but there are many theories that have evolved. This chapter won't be able to answer the question on why we dream, but this chapter will help to explain to you what your dreams could mean.

A Little about Dreaming:

Dreams occur when you're asleep, but most dreams happen in REM, and this is where the most vivid dreams occur. REM means rapid eye movement, and this is the part of sleep where our brain is most active. You may only remember one dream at best, but it's been determined that people usually dream about four to six times each night. This gives you multiple chances each night to become lucid in your dream.

Dreams are important to your wellbeing and health, and a lot of research has been done. There was one study done where patients were woken up before they hit REM, and this caused depression, anxiety, and a lack of coordination, tendencies to hallucinate, weight gain, and an increase in tension. This has led many people to believe that dreams help you to incorporate memories, solve problems that are posed in real life, and even experience your own emotions.

Sigmund Freud did research about dreams as well, saying that it opens us up to our own subconscious. According to Freud, dreams helped to reveal what a person is thinking, what their motivations are, and even helps people to understand their unconscious desires. He says that it allows people to act on urges that they wouldn't feel comfortable acting on in normal society.

What Dreams Mean:

Different people believe different things on what dreams mean and even why we dream. Some experts even believe that dreams don't have an actually connection with our real lives. There are other experts that argue it connects us to our fears, concerns, desires, feelings, and problems that we feel we have. Interpreting your dreams is said to help people to gain insight into their own lives, helping them in the waking world. This section will help to shed a little more light on the subject so that you can form your own opinion.

Some research shows that dreams may be how we form memories. Other studies say that during the time we are awake we learn new things, and so while we're dreaming, we're able to take short term memories and make them long term memories.

While some argue that we dream to create memories, others argue that they are just a way to sort out the emotions that we're feeling at night, your brain is said to slow down, and while you're sleeping, you're able to cycle through your emotions and sort those that you felt during the day. If you fear that you're about to be laid off, you may not concentrate on that during the day. Instead, you'll concentrate on everyday tasks, but at night, this fear will manifest in the form of a small nightmare or just a dream that relates to your fear.

There is, of course, a theory that says that dreams are pointless. Many people disagree, and this book will concentrate on how dreams are important in your lives. The brain is extremely complex, but simply because we don't know the exact reason we dream doesn't mean that they have no importance. There are endless possibilities and answers that we may one day discover.

Your Brain as You Dream:

Before you can truly understand the meaning in your dreams, you might want to take a look at what happens to your brain while you dream. You go through five stages of sleep when you go to bed, and the first is known as light sleep. It's extremely easy to wake up when you're in 'light sleep'. Then you move to the second stage, allowing you to move a little deeper into your slumber. At stage three and four, you're at your deepest sleep where your brain is slowing down. You'll experience brain activities which are called delta brain waves and after about ninety minutes, you slip into REM, which is your fifth stage of sleep.

REM was discovered in 1953 by Eugene Aserinsky, and it was characterized by the way that your eyes move during your sleep in the fifth stage. During REM you'll experience an increase in your heart rate, breathing, and you'll even have your blood pressure raise. The rest of your body is essentially paralyzed until you can slip out of REM. It's at this phase that your body will create dreams that you cycle into.

Some Dream Facts:

Humans aren't actually the only species that experiences REM. Even animals such as elephants and dogs experience it. It is said that when an animal sleeps standing up, such as an elephants, then they aren't in REM. However, in the case of the elephant, it is believed that when they are lying down, they are in REM. You can usually tell when your dog is in REM because they exhibit signs of dreaming, such as whimpering or running in their sleep.

When people are snoring, they are also not dreaming. The noise would interrupt the sleep cycle, keeping them from reaching REM. Another fun fact is that people who have been blind since birth still experience dreams. However, the dreams form around their other senses such as touch, smell, and sound. People can dream in color as well, but originally people thought that we could only dream in black and white.

Dreams will last anywhere from five to twenty minutes for most people. Most people will actually not remember every time that they dream. It is believed that throughout our lives we spend about six years in our dreams, which is a lot of time to experience what you want in the world if you learn to control your dreams through lucid dreaming.

A Little about Recalling Dreams:

Dreams are mysterious to many experts still, and that's one reason that they can't understand why people forget their dreams so easily. There are many theories, including that we're just designed that way. It is thought that if we could remember our dreams in vivid details as we experience them that we would have a hard time distinguishing dreams from reality.

During REM, most of our systems are shut down, and so our brain can't turn back on until certain brain activities happen. Other people believe that we don't really forget our dreams. Instead, they think we don't have the capability to access them. Researchers believe that all of our dreams are stored in our brains but that we can't access the memories. This is one of the reasons that they believe some people will remember a dream once it has been triggered in the waking world.

Here Are Some Ways to Recall Dreams:

- **Remind Yourself:** You can remind yourself of your dream by making it a conscious decision. Before actually laying down to sleep, try to tell yourself in your head that you want to remember what you're going to dream. By making this conscious decision as you fall asleep, you usually can remember more come morning.

- **Don't Use an Alarm:** If you skip the alarm, you're more likely to remember your dreams as well. Waking up naturally will help you to focus on what you've experience when alarms make it hard to focus on anything but starting your morning and why you need to get up.

- **Repeat Your Dream:** When you wake up, try to think about what you were dreaming. You should be able to start replaying the memory in your head or even say it out loud. This will help you to remember the dream later on. Writing it down is also a great way to remember details.

How to Enhance Your Lucid Dreams

If you want to lucid dream, then you're in luck. There are things that you can do to enhance your lucid dreams, and they range from diet to supplements that can help. Intensifying, remembering, and staying aware of your dreams is important to having them help you in your day to day life.

Pay Attention to Your Diet:

Your diet has a lot to do with how you dream, and making sure that you have B6 is a great dream booster. Tryptophan is a dream booster as well, and if you increase your intake of these supplements, then your dreams will likely be more vivid, filled with more emotion and color. Some of the food are tuna, shrimp, salmon and even in chicken. Tofu, kidney beans, and pumpkin seeds can help as well. You should try to have these foods in your life more. A paleo diet can help with lucid dreaming as well.

Supplements & Herbs:

Asparagus root is a great herbal medicine if you want to increase lucid dreaming. It's been used by shamans and monks as Chinese herbal medicine, allowing you to tap into your visions while you sleep. You can consume it directly as a root or even in tea. Valerian root is also known to help because it is a muscle relaxant that has a calming affect, helping you to lucid dream. It can also cause a deep sleep which will help you to recall your dreams better. It's usually best to have it in tea form. Mugwort is another herb that is known to help you with your dreams, and it can enhance your dreams, helping you to have more vivid and prolonged dreams. It can be smoked in a pipe or taken as a tea.

Medication to Help:

Galantamine is a medication that is often associated with lucid dreaming, and it can also help to treat Alzheimer's disease or any other disease that impairs memory. It has history in both ancient Greece and China, enhancing your mental awareness. It's a combination of snowdrop plants, lilies, and daffodil. It encourages the production of acetylcholine, which is associated with both dreams and memory. It can lengthen the dreams and help you to recall them. However, it does have side effects and some of them are a loss of appetite, diarrhea and nausea. It can also cause sleep paralysis. You shouldn't take it if you have liver problems, heart issues, kidney issues or asthma. No matter what medication that you take to help with lucid dreaming, make sure to seek professional consultation with your doctor.

Why You Want to Remember Dreams

You'll find that there are many reasons you'd want to remember your dreams, and chances are you already do want to remember them if you're reading this book. Dreams have many benefits to your day to day life in the waking world.

It Gives You Help with Decision Making:

If you're having an issue dealing with any particular situation, then a good night's sleep can help you to make a decision. Your dreams will shed light on anything that you're trying to find a solution to, and it can help you by showing how you really feel. It can even shed light on any health concerns you may be having. This can also help you to deal with the stress happening your daily life, providing you a solution to that much stress.

They Let You See Your Subconscious:

Your dreams are a way to look into your subconscious since your conscious mind can't remember everything your brain processes during the day. You make sense of your day through your dreams, so it'll help you to understand your surroundings. This will allow you to consciously analyze the information in your dreams, and when you wake up, you'll have more insight on how you feel. It will also help to teach you to analyze the waking world as well, making it easier to move through life consciously.

You'll Become a More Self-Aware Person:

Dreams are considered to be an extension of yourself, so if you don't like what you see in your dreams then you know something needs to change in your life. They can work as a way to motivate you into doing the things you want, and nightmares are often negative messages that will help you to analyze what you're doing. Dreams are positive for your psychological health. Too many nightmares may be because you're too stressed or anxious. If you're denying this fact in the waking world, your dreams will give you the proper insight on it.

Starting to Analyze Your Dreams

Some people are okay with being able to move on with dreams, unable to remember them, and dismissing anything that is too odd. However, this isn't great for everyone. Many people want to understand what their dreams mean and what their unconscious mind is trying to tell them. You can understand your tendencies and habits by analyzing your dreams, and it can help to shed light on your personality. You should understand yourself, and if you want to connect with your inner self, improve yourself, and figure out ways to solve your conflicts, then your dreams can help.

Ways to Analyze Your Dreams:

There are different ways that you can help to analyze your dreams. You already learned how to remember them a little better, and that's half the battle.

- **Write Down Your Dreams:** Writing down your dreams is extremely important if you want to analyze them. Writing your dreams down can help you to remember details that your mind would forget about otherwise. The first few minutes of waking up is extremely important, as most people forget their dreams in this time period. When you're waking up, your brain is considered to be logical and rational, putting you in a completely different mindset than when you're dreaming. When dreaming, you're indulging your irrational and creative side. When you're awake, your conscious mind may even try to fill in gaps that were in your dream to make it logical. This is why you need to take the time to write it down immediately because the longer you've been awake, the longer your brain has to try to twist your dream into making it much more logical. Try to keep from writing the whole story when you're recording your dreams. Just write down whatever fragments you can, including any images that you have. You don't need to put a sequence to the events, as the sequence is much less important in analyzing your dreams. The symbols, as you'll learn later, are considered to be much more important.

- **Pay Attention to People:** Paying attention to people and relationships in dreams is extremely important. It is important to remember that you can direct your dream, but knowing the relationship you have with the person in the dream is important. If you dream about someone you have a direct relationship to, then there isn't much to question. Though, if you dream about someone that you don't know, it's likely that the person you're dreaming about represents a part of yourself or the problem that you're dealing with.

- **Pay Attention to Image Association:** When dreaming, you'll want to consider images that appear in your dream. Try to think about what your conscious mind might be trying to present you with the symbols that you're seeing. Take a look at your surroundings first, and the first question that you should ask yourself is if you think you've ever been in that area before in the waking world. Afterwards, you'll want to see if there was anything odd that stood out. A symbol doesn't mean something written somewhere. It can be an animal that stood out to you, a tree that seemed out of place, or anything that you took note of that seemed off. Trust your instincts when you're looking for symbols. Ask yourself after you identify what they could be, what possible meanings they have. What does the symbol mean to you? Write it down, and don't be afraid if there is more than one possible meaning. Our brains are complex, and it'd be odd if there was only one meaning that you could think of.

- **Take a Look at Emotions:** In your dreams you'll have emotions as well, and you need to pay attention to them. Even if your dreams aren't lucid, you should have emotion in your dreams. There may be more of an 'emotional tone' rather than a direct emotion. In the waking world, it's easy to tell that you're angry. It may not be as easy to tell that you're angry in your dream. You may see more red, things may be dryer and more uncomfortable, but there should always be something that tips you off to what emotion you're experiencing. Ask yourself what feelings you experienced in your dreams or if you had any pain while experiencing your dreams.

- **Look for Connections:** The biggest connection that you should look for is if your dream connects with your day or not. Also referred to as 'day residue', you may have connections in your dreams to what happened in your life. For example, if you run into someone that day, you're more likely to dream about them. If you had trouble with a stapler, you may see more staplers in your dream. This is simply because these figures and objects are in your mind.

- **Ask The Right Question:** One of the best questions to ask yourself is if your dream is trying to tell you something. Asking this question opens you up to possibility, which will help you to understand what your dream was saying. Dreams are not under your conscious control, and so you will not be able to anticipate them or will them to happen. Dreaming might be an autonomous function. Ask yourself if your subconscious mind is trying to expose something to you. Just keep in mind that there isn't usually one particular answer.

- **Going Back to Symbols:** You need to look at symbols once more, and you'll learn more about symbols later in this book. There are symbols that have common meanings throughout dreams, and once you learn these, you'll want to look for them in your dreams as well.

Understanding Preparation Essentials

This chapter will teach you different dream methods and how they can help you personally. However, before you can learn that, you need to learn some basic components that need to be understood. The first one is sleep interruption. This is a process when a patient is awake on purpose during their normal sleep period, and then they fall asleep soon after. A silent alarm is usually best because it'll bring a person slightly into consciousness, but it'll keep them from becoming fully conscious. Drinking a lot of water before you sleep is another common method. This will force you to get up and use the restroom, which will interrupt your natural sleep pattern.

Sleep continuity is another term that you'll need to understand. Some people struggle to go to sleep and stay asleep. If you're having trouble falling asleep, avoid water or liquids for an hour before you go to bed. This will keep it where you don't have to get up and go to the restroom, which won't interrupt your sleep pattern. It's also best to avoid caffeine and sugar before you go to sleep as well because this will often disrupt your sleep pattern. Though, caffeine is known to stimulate your brain as well. If you aren't sensitive to caffeine, then it can actually help you to induce a lucid dream as well.

Reality checks are the last principle that you'll need to understand before you're ready to get into dream methods. Reality checks are tests that you perform both while dreaming and when awake. You should make it a habit, and it'll increase your chance of having a lucid dream. One of the best examples of a reality check is in the movie "Inception" where the top doesn't stop spinning if he's in a dream. You repeat an action so much in reality, but it should have a different effect in your dreams because your dream world is different.

Some Reality Check Ideas:

Here are some reality check ideas that might help you to find something that works for you.

- **Jumping:** When you're awake, you'll want to jump. You're always going to land when you're awake. However, when you're dreaming, you can do the same thing, but you're more likely to float back down. You'll usually be able to notice a difference.

- **Powers:** You can check for powers while you're awake, which is comical to think about. However, you can manifest powers in your dream. For example, try walking through a wall, changing shape, or flying. Heat vision is another power that people often use as their reality check.

- **Study Your Hands:** You'll want to study your hands, and once you are asleep, check your hands again. Check to see if they look odd to you. You may not be able to see a strange color, too many fingers, or abnormalities, but if you know your own hands well enough, you should notice that something is off.

- **Physics:** You can use your hands by testing to see if you can push your fingers through your hand in real life. When you do this in your dreams, you'll be able to. In real life, it obviously will not work.

- **Identity:** Once you are in your dream, you can check for your identity as well. Are you the same age? Are you the same gender? Do you have the same relationships to people? If you come across a false negative, where you thought you weren't the same age and then you suddenly feel like it's changed, then this is most likely a dream as well.

For reality checks to work, you need to use them often while you're waking. It has to become a routine so that you remember to practice them in your dreams as well. You should also perform this check as soon as you wake up as well. People can think they wake up and then they're dreaming. Setting an alarm can help with false awakenings as well. Make sure that no matter what check you use that it is fast, discreet and reliable. You certainly don't want to embarrass yourself in person.

Preparing Your Body:

You can actually prepare your body to get a good night's sleep as well. One way to do so is to exercise during the day. Of course, you shouldn't exercise about here hours before bed. The best time to exercise is in the morning or afternoon. Exercise stimulates your body, but at this time, it's unlikely that it'll keep you up. If you're still having an issue falling asleep, then you can try to read before bed. Reading about lucid dreaming is also a great way to get your-self ready. Some people believe that this will help you to increase your chances of experiencing a lucid dream at night.

Some Dream Methods

You're all prepped, but with this method, you'll need to be able to start working on the different dream methods to induce lucid dreaming. You'll find four different methods in this chapter. Keep in mind that different methods work best for different people.

The Mild Method:

MILD actually stands for "Mnemonic Induction of Lucid Dreams", and the technique was actually created by Stephen LaBerge. Stephen LaBerge is the author of "Exploring the World of Lucid Dreaming". This method is supposed to work as you fall asleep. Concentrate on the intention of falling asleep, which means that you should remember the process of falling asleep when you enter your dream. With this method, many people prefer a mantra before they go to bed. The mantra can be personal to you, such as "I'll remember this dream" or even "I will be aware the next time I dream". Try to remember your last dream, and then add the mantra to it while you think about the last dream before bed. You don't have to repeat this mantra out loud, but make sure that you're prominently thinking about it as you fall asleep.

You can repeat this mantra if you wake up from the middle of a dream at night as well. Just repeat it every time you wake up, jotting down what you can, and then try to go back to sleep. This method is considered to be extremely simple, but many people find it too boring to keep it in their mind for long. This is great for people who have a good memory, as it'll make it easier for them to remember any future intentions that they had even in their dreams.

The VILD Method:

VILD stands for "Visually Incubated Lucid Dreams", and this method requires your body to be completely relaxed. Make sure that you empty your brain before you go to sleep. Many people find it's helpful if you read before bed, and make sure that you get to the point where you are extremely tired. When you hit that point, visualize a dream that you've prepared before you go to sleep. Try to visualize every detail of the dream that you want to have. Add in a friend, an object, and make sure that you even have your setting chosen before you to go to bed. You'll also need to choose reality checks to perform when you start to dream.

When you are ready, start to visualize your dream. Do it again and again, before you actually fall asleep. Keep your thoughts in mind as you fall asleep. If your thoughts begin to drift while you fall asleep, ignore any irrelevant thoughts and put your mind back on your goal so that your subconscious will concentrate on these desires. Make sure that you don't give up. If you do this method properly, you should drift into the dream that you have planned out for yourself. This is why it is extremely important that you have your reality checks ready for when you're in the world of your dreams to make sure you don't mistake it for reality.

The VILD method is extremely beneficial and easy for most people. Of course, it's not for everyone. Some people can't get to sleep because they are concentrating too much on visualizing, and this method isn't good for those people. Just remember to have reality checks so that your reality and dream world is kept completely separate.

The WILD Method:

WILD stands for "Wake Initiated Lucid Dreaming", and it is another method to induce lucid dreaming. This method, like any other method, isn't for everyone. This method includes falling asleep as a conscious decision. It's similar to self-hypnosis, and many people actually believe this method induces an astral projection instead of a lucid dream. This method is considered easier by many people because they can perform it early in the morning once they've woken up and have time to spare. This will keep the sleep cycle continuing with a normal REM period.

If you want this method to work, you will have to be relaxed. You have to lay down, and practice tensing and relaxing up and then relaxing your body from there. Start from your shoulders, working your way down to your toes. Once you've finished at your toes, then you'll want to make your way back up to your head. When done, if done properly, your body should feel relaxed but also slightly happy. Once this is completely, make sure you pay attention to your real body. If you pay attention, you'll be able to enter a sleep paralysis when done properly.

However, even in sleep paralysis, you shouldn't actually lose the ability to be aware of your body. This feeling may be unpleasant to some people, and some people have reported at tingling or even a buzzing sensation going through their body. Some people say it feels even worse, but to most people the feeling isn't that bad. You shouldn't be worried, as it's a natural occurrence when you fall asleep to feel this way as well.

There are advantages to the WILD method, which will allow you to consciously lucid dream. However, one of the biggest disadvantages of this dream method is that it takes many people a long time to master this method. You'll need more dedication, and you'll need more patience. Doing this the first couple of times may even be frightening for some people. Just keep in mind that it's completely safe, and it can work for anyone if they put in enough effort.

The WBTB Method:

WBTB stands for "Wake Back to Bed" method. With this method, you'll be waking yourself up from four to six hours of sleep. Once you're awake, you'll then lie-down back again and after a few minutes go back to bed. At this time, while you're awake at least, you'll want to do something that relates to lucid dreaming. This method should be modified to fit you personally if you are sleeping too deeply to become lucid. Try to sleep in a different area once you go back to bed. For example, you might want a different bed, chair, or to even sleep on the floor to keep you from sleeping too deeply. Changing the way you sleep can help as well, such as sleeping with different covers, a different pillow, or just in a different direction. You should teach your body to be more conscious of your sleeping habits.

The biggest advantage of this method is that it is reliable to induce lucid dreaming, and it can even be combined with other methods. However, the disadvantage is that it will disrupt your sleep cycle. If you wake up a lot during the night anyways, then this method might be perfect for you. If you're used to sleeping through the night, then this might not be the right method.

A Little on Nightmares

Dreams have a habit of becoming terrifying from time to time, and it's normal for anyone to have nightmares. Some people have even woken up in the middle of the night screaming, others will wake up with their heart beating too quickly or even wake up in a cold sweat. If this happens, then you've probably had a nightmare, even if you can't remember it. At one time, people believed that adults would outgrow nightmares, but this isn't proven. Many adults suffer nightmares.

The problem with nightmares is that they are realistic just like lucid dreaming, and it can make them appear to be extremely disturbing. Some nightmares are so bad that they will wake you up from sleeping as well. Nightmares occurring during REM, are just like lucid dreaming as well. That isn't uncommon because REM is where dreams mostly occur. Nightmares commonly occur closer to morning because REM sleep becomes longer the longer you sleep.

Night terrors are another type of nightmares, but they'll usually occur within the first few hours that you sleep. Night terrors are often less realistic, and you may not know exactly what you were afraid of when you wake up. Nightmares are personal, and so just because two people have nightmares, it's unlikely that they're terrified of the same things.

Some Likely Causes:

Dreaming is a mystery to many scientists, and this is why it's hard to pinpoint why people are suffering nightmares as well. The belief is that nightmares are caused by many different issues. For example, some people will get nightmares if they eat too close to bedtime. Other people will suffer nightmares due to medication, but others get nightmares because they suffer depression, anxiety, PTSD, or have lived through other traumas. Nightmares can commonly trigger sleep disorders, including restless leg syndrome and even sleep apnea.

Some Treatment:

There are treatments for nightmares, but it doesn't always get rid of them. Luckily, proper treatment will usually at least lessen the frequency that people suffer nightmares. The first thing that you should do if you experience nightmares is to ask your doctor if it could be a side effect of any medication that you're on. If you determine that they are not medication related, then you'll want to look to see if there are any behavioral changes that can be made to get rid of them.

If you deal with PTSD, trauma, anxiety or depression, then you may want to see a psychologist. Imagery rehearsal treatment helps to change nightmares by telling your-self how they want to change. By visualizing a different outcome, you can change the outcome of your nightmare. This gives you a way to take control over your own fears. Keeping a regular sleep schedule can also reduce the number of nightmares that you experience. Another way to help with nightmares is to exercise on a daily basis. Even yoga or meditation will help as well, and you'll want to practice good sleep hygiene. Preventing sleep deprivation will help, and make sure that your bedroom is relaxing. You shouldn't relate your bedroom to stressful activities if you want to sleep peacefully. If your nightmares have a reoccurring symbol, then you may want to interpret the nightmare to make it go away.

Creating an Atmosphere for Your Bedroom:

By creating the right atmosphere for your bedroom, you're much less likely to have nightmares. A calm and conducive atmosphere will not only help you with positive dreams, but it'll help you with lucid dreaming as well. Here are a few ways to make the atmosphere in your bedroom just right, and it can be done by anyone.

- **Aromatherapy:** The way your room smells can actually change the way that you dream. You don't want your room to smell unpleasant in any way. You want to have something that's calming in your room. To do this, you can use candles and incense, but you'll find that there are some you should use and some you shouldn't. Keep in mind that you don't want scents that will keep you energized and awake such as lemongrass. You want calming scents that are pleasing to you. Many people use rose oil, lavender, or even chamomile. Vanilla and orange are also known to help relax you and sooth your thoughts. Opening a window in the room can help as well, though. You'll find that fresh air can help you to let go of negativity that's hanging over you.

- **Music:** Soothing music will inspire good dreams and help you to fall asleep faster. Of course, music doesn't mean you have to put on your favorite band or instrumental music. It can also, at least in this case, refer to white noise. This can help to relax your mind and drive away stress. Of course, if you use music then you should have a timer where it'll switch off. You don't need something that plays constantly throughout the night. Singing bowls are also a great way to introduce noise into your room that will help you to sleep. The vibrations that these produce will help your mind to relax so that you fall asleep faster.

- **Positions:** There are some scientists that believe that if you lay on your back you have a higher chance of having a nightmare, which would lower your chance of lucid dreaming. It's best to try to find a position that is comfortable to you that won't have you laying on your back which would keep your mind on full alert. You can fall into sleep paralysis much more easily if you're lying on your back. Sleep paralysis is where your brain has put your body to sleep but somehow the mind still remains awake. It's a glitch that can be terrifying if you experience it. It can also occur the other way around where your mind wakes up before your body but your body hasn't gotten the signal to wake up yet.

- **Lighting:** Light in your room when you're sleeping can be counterproductive. You'll have better dreams as well as better luck with lucid dreams when you don't have light bothering you while you're laying down. Some people do wish to have a nightlight, and that's fine, but you need to be mindful. You shouldn't have something that is more than five percent lighting if you're using it in this manner. Mood lighting will help most often, but just make sure that it's something that you can fall asleep without difficulty in. if you're exposed to light when sleeping, it's more likely that your sleep is shallow and easily broken. It's a natural response to wake up to light, and it can interfere with lucid dreaming quite a bit.

Common Nightmare Interpretations:

Of course, just like you can interpret dreams, you can interpret nightmares as well. Below you'll find a few common symbols in your nightmares and a small explanation behind them.

- **Malformation:** Malformation as well as injury is commonly found in a nightmare. You'll often be wounded, and it's a way for your brain to let you know that you have some issues that you'll need to address. It could be due to feeling vulnerable or weak, and these symbols can be due to you or your friends. However, there are more specific symbols as well, such as broken bones. Broken bones can mean that you're trying to break free of something or you feel that something is broken in your life. It can even show that you need to mend something in your life.

- **Alien:** If you're having nightmares about aliens, it could mean that you're feeling as if you don't' know the people around you anymore. It can also show you that you don't know different parts of yourself, and your subconscious is usually trying to warn you that you need to accept yourself in order to grow as a person.

- **Broken Teeth/Teeth Falling Out:** If you are having nightmares about your teeth, this is actually common. It ties into insecurity, worry, and often it signifies a great deal of anxiety. If you have teeth that are falling out, it could be due to a lack of confidence. It can show a lack of communication or a difficulty in communication in certain situations. It can also be a way for your subconscious to berate you over saying something you feel you shouldn't have said, symbolizing that your words will one day haunt you.

- **Death:** Death will be covered more in depth in a later chapter, but it's often a reflection of a fear over someone. If you fear for your life, then you should look at the situations that you're putting yourself in in the waking world, even if they aren't exactly deadly.

- **Drowning:** If you dream about drowning, then you're terrified and feeling overwhelmed. You may also be feeling trapped, but it could be that you're trapped by yourself as well. Your own emotions can trap you in the waking world. On the other hand, this could be a sign of rebirth as well, such as waking up from the dream means that you'll wake up from that terror. It can also show that you're having issues with your own emotions.

- **Natural Disasters:** This is more uncommon for nightmares, but you'll find that people do have nightmares about natural disasters. You have to be extremely emotionally charged to have these types of dreams. If you're dreaming about a volcanic eruption, then you're likely to have pent up rage and anger. This could signify that you're willing to blow up and that you're just at your tipping point. Earthquakes often show that your routine is disrupted and you feel as if your foundation is breaking apart. Hurricanes and tornados usually show emotional tension due to situations that you need to address in the waking world.

- **Bugs:** If you're having nightmares about bugs, such as spiders or other insects, then it's likely that you have something small holding you back. You often have an annoyance building up into anger in this case. These insects can also represent people that are bugging you and holding you back in the waking world. Spiders can often mean that you're caught in a trap or 'web' that you don't know how to get out of.

- **Dead People:** If you're dreaming about dead people, you may just be afraid of death. You may also be having nightmares due to feeling as if someone is going to die without problems being resolved. It may tell you that you're killing someone with your actions and words, but if you see yourself dead, your subconscious may be trying to tell you that you're dying from your own habits and circumstances as well.

Other Ways to Stave off Nightmares:

You need the proper mindset to stave off nightmares. No matter if you keep the right lifestyle, including proper diet and exercise, there are still things in your life that can cause you to have nightmares. You can't keep nightmares away from ever, but keeping the right mindset will help. Below you'll find what can help you keep the right mindset so that nightmares don't set in.

- **Images:** It's important that you try to keep away from gory images because they can often cause nightmares. Everyone loves TV shows or movies that has gore every once in a while, but you need to know that you're exposing yourself to nightmares when you watch them. It's best to avoid them whenever possible, and you should also avoid using your cell phone right before bed as well. Being exposed to "blue light" which comes from the screen of your phone can disrupt your dreams, so keeping away from this blue light about an hour before bed will help you to sleep better.

- **Issues:** If you aren't dealing with the issues in your own family, then you'll likely go to bed unhappy. This is true with any relationship in your life, so it's important that you try to talk out issues and express how you're really feeling before you go to bed to try to avoid nightmares.

- **Work:** It's important that you don't work right before bed because it'll just raise your stress levels and cause tension. This interferes with your sleep which can far too easily lead to nightmares. Try to finish your work about an hour or two before you actually try to go to sleep.

Some Common Meanings

Many people believe that dreams are a way for your unconscious mind to tell you something, and that's why dream interpretation is so important to many people. In this chapter, we'll go over symbolic meanings in common dreams. Once you can identify an issue and some universal definitions, you may get a better idea of what your dreams mean. However, make sure to read into the whole dream so that you can understand the personal meaning that your mind is trying to tell you. Just remember that sometimes a symbol, especially one that is personal to you, will have a personal meaning.

Dreams of Flying:

This is one of the happier dreams that you may be experiencing, but they have meaning to them usually as well. You'll find many common meanings for flying below.

- **Feeling in Control:** If you feel in control in your life, then it's common to be flying at ease. Of course, if you're enjoying the view, then you may feel as if you have a good grasp on the situation. Flying can show you a personal sense of power.

- **Self-Esteem:** If you feel as if you have power when you fly, this could be a good reflection on your self-esteem. This could mean that you are looking down at people because you feel as if you are finally better than those around you. Of course, it's important to stay humble.

- **Feeling Free:** If you feel as if you've just experienced freedom, then this is another positive reason that you could be dreaming of flying. This can leave you with a positive feeling of being motivated as well.

Dreams of Being Naked:

If you commonly have dreams where you're naked in a proper place or not, then that also has some meaning. A fear of nakedness or being exposed is one of the most common reasons, but you'll find that there are other reasons as well.

- **Phobia:** If you fear being exposed or being naked, then you may dream of being naked often. If you are feeling ashamed, then you may be having these dreams as well. It could be that you're embarrassed over something that you feel or how you are as well. Clothes allow you to conceal, but you can hide who you are based on what you wear, especially in your dreams. Of course, when you're naked, then you aren't able to hide anything any longer.

- **Not Feeling Prepared:** If you feel like you aren't prepared, then you may dream about being naked during something extremely important. This could be going to school naked, giving a presentation naked, or just doing any activity that you're worried about while being completely exposed.

- **Feeling Arrogant:** Most people don't know, but if you're extremely arrogant, then you'll often be fine being completely nude. Of course, this may mean that you look down on others, and so you'll need to be more humble. This only applies if you aren't feeling out of place being naked in your dream.

- **Feeling Vulnerable:** If you are naked, then you're now vulnerable to the world. This could show that you fear being helpless, and you may have trouble letting your guard down as well. You'll need to look at how you view yourself and see if there is any insecurity that you don't want to expose. You'll often fear that people are criticizing as well, but it's often just in your head.

Dreams of Falling:

Another common dream is falling, and it can be a general sense of falling, falling from a cliff, from an airplane, or even just a building. It's common to believe that if you die in your dream that you'll die in your life, but this just isn't Tue. Many people fall in their dreams, and some people even die after the fall. They wake up just fine, so there is no need for too much fear. Some of the common reasons for dreams of falling are below.

- **Lack of Control:** When you're falling, you can't control anything, and this can reflect your own life. If you're having these dreams often, then this can be a clear indication that you feel stressed out and overwhelmed in the waking world. You'll want to look at your life, looking at your home life, work, and even in your relationships. Ask yourself if there is something that you can't control or if there's something bothering you.

- **Feeling Insecure:** If you feel insecure, then you may feel unstable and have falling dreams as well. It can also denote a lack of confidence, and this can be due to any aspect of your life. You may be worried about losing something dear to you, including people, your home, or even your job. If you feel as if you lack the ability to measure up to someone's expectation of you, then this could mean that falling signifies that you feel you're letting someone down as well.

Dreams about Food:

When you're dreaming about food, it often signifies that you feel that you need more nourishment and energy in your life. Food nourishes your body, but your brain is actually telling you that you need to nourish your mind, which means food dreams directly relate to your intellect, spiritual power, inner feelings, abilities, emotions and thoughts. Make sure to analyze what food you're eating. If you're eating junk food, then your mind may be telling you that you're lacking what you need to nourish your mind and make healthier changes in your day to day life.

Dreams about Cheating:

The truth that many people don't want to admit to is that almost everyone dreams about cheating at one point in their life or another. Cheating dreams can be so real that you may even wake up, feeling as if you or your spouse has actually cheated. Of course, you'll need to settle down. It's natural for these dreams to be highly unsettling, but these dreams are usually a reflection of your own insecurity. These dreams are often trying to tell you something about yourself, and you'll find some possibilities below...

- **Poor Self-Esteem:** Poor self-esteem and a lack of trust can cause you to have these dreams as well. If you ever feel as if you aren't deserving of your partner, then you may start to fear that you'll be cheated on. This is a reflection of how you view your self-worth, and in your dream the person may be more successful, prettier or some other characteristic about yourself that you feel isn't good enough for your partner. Healthy relationships have a healthy foundation of trust.

- **Feeling Guilty:** If you are the one that's cheating, then you may actually be feeling guilty over something. If you haven't told your partner that you're unhappy, if you're being dishonest, if you're feeling unhappy in your relationship due to your partner and you're staying silent, or if you're looking at other people, then this could be causing it. However, it can also be a sign of a quality that you want, such as authority, control, or even power.

- **Being Abandoned:** If you're dreaming about being cheated on, then you may have a fear of abandonment. It can also show that you're concerned about where the future is going or if your loved one is true or will be there for you throughout your life. If you're waiting for commitment, this can lead to that type of fear as well.

Dreams of Death:

If you're dreaming about death, it quickly turns into a nightmare. This can be even more disturbing if you're dreaming about someone that you love or if you're dreaming about you dying as well. You'll have to look closely at symbolism to know what these dreams mean.

- **Coping:** If you're dreaming about someone you love dying or yourself dying, then you are probably coping with the reality of death. Death is inevitable, and it can be hard to ignore. It's even harder to ignore when you're asleep. Of course, if a loved one is in the hospital, ill, or aging, then dreams of dying may be more relevant as well. If you are sick or in the hospital, these dreams can occur as well.

- **Self-Growth:** If you're dreaming about yourself dying or someone that is like you, then this could represent the death of old habits. It can also be a part of you that suppressed, but this is only if you are dreaming about someone that looks like you or yourself. Of course, if you're dreaming about someone you know dying, it could be because they have changed as well. Your feelings for that person may have changed or disappeared altogether as well. If you are a mother and are dreaming of children dying, then this may be an indicator that you need to let your children live their own lives. Of course, if you aren't a mother, then it may represent your own inner child passing as well.

- **Dreaming of Loved Ones**: If you're dreaming of a loved one that has passed recently, this may be a coping mechanism. It may also mean that you didn't get to say everything that you wanted to that person. Of course, if someone has been dead for a while, it could just be that something in your life reminds you of that person. For example, if you're dreaming about relationship issues and your dead grandmother, then it may be because you think your grandmother could give you practical insight and advice.

Dreams of Being Chased:

Many people experience dreams of being chased, and this is common to go with feelings of anxiety, especially if you are experiencing anxiety in the waking world. Of course, the question you should be asking yourself is what you're running from in your dream. Sadly, in many of these dreams, you may not even know what you're running away from. It's completely natural to want to run away from something that scares you or even makes you uncomfortable. Here are a few more things that a dream of being chased could mean.

- **Fear:** If your dream deals with an attacker, then this may tell you that you want to run away from someone that is making you feel uncomfortable. Of course, if you feel physically vulnerable, then this reason is much more likely.

- **You're Chasing:** If you're the one that's chasing after something, then this could represent a drive to get something done. Your subconscious mind may be telling you to run after what you want. However, it can also mean that you feel as if you're falling behind in your life. Just remember that your dreams are based on your subconscious mind, and so you need to pay attention for any other symbols you may see as well.

- **Fear of Yourself:** If you can, try to check out who is attacking you. Does the person remind you of yourself? If they do, then it might actually symbolize that you're trying to run away from yourself. This could be because they have a physical attribute like you, or you may just have an emotional or 'gut' feeling. You may feel anger, jealousy, or fear manifesting, and this may mean that you need to confront something about yourself that you don't' want to.

- **Avoidance:** One way to look at these dreams is that you're trying to avoid a problem in the waking world. Running away turns into a coping mechanism to deal with this fear and stressor. If you tend to run away from issues, then these dreams are much more likely.

Dreams & Meditation

Meditation and dreams are not the same thing, but you'll find that they can go hand in hand. Meditation is a practice that has been along for an extremely long time, and it has many mental benefits that have been time tested and proven as well. It helps you to relieve the stress that you're feeling in your life, and therefore it can lead to more tranquility and peace both in the waking world and in your dreams. This can help you to combat your negative emotions, and it can help you to relieve any bad dreams that you may be having. The reason people mediate is in hopes of delving into their conscious mind and their subconscious.

Meditation is supposed to help you get more in tune with how you feel, and your subconscious is how you'll find your dream patterns. If you have positive thoughts in your subconscious, then positive dreams will follow shortly after. If negative thoughts are clouding your subconscious, bad experiences and nightmares are soon to follow. You can't have a constant negative subconscious or a constant positive subconscious. It just isn't possible, but you need to reduce the amount of negative in your subconscious as much as possible if you don't want to suffer from bad dreams on a regular basis, and that's where meditation is helpful.

During the meditation process, you can drive away your negative feelings as well as your negative thoughts. However, you need to see meditation as a lifestyle choice because you'll need to be persistent with your efforts. You can't just give up the moment your negative dreams go away because they will come back. Meditation works best when you can set time aside for it at least every other day. To start meditation you need to set the right mood for it so that you have the right frame of mind.

By creating the right mood, you're increasing the benefits that you can reap through meditation by making sure that it is always done properly. You should have the right atmosphere in the spot you pick, and make sure that you have at least twenty minutes to spare because you shouldn't meditate for any less time. Of course, keep in mind that meditation sessions can be longer, especially if you are trying to deal with something particular in your life.

Heartbeat Meditation:

In this meditation, you're going to need to focus on your heartbeat. By focusing on your heartbeat, you're able to tune everything else out and clear your mind. Your heartbeat is thought to have hidden powers, but you can use it to give yourself relief. You need to use it to clear away mental stress, and you have to use this type of meditation using the steps below.

Steps:

1. Sit in a comfortable position, but you can sit any way that you want to. It doesn't have to be any particular pose. Now start by breathing in deeply, placing your hand over your heart.

2. Next you'll want to close your eyes, visualizing that your heartbeat is starting to vibrate through to your hand.

3. You'll then need to visualize that your heartbeat is pulsing to the rest of your body. Imagine that your heartbeat is nourishing

your body, and it should leave you feeling refreshed.

This meditation should be done about two to three times each week.

Kundalini Meditation:

This is a meditational practice that is meant to cleanse yourself, but it does refer to feminine power. However, that doesn't mean that this is a sexist meditation. It just means to refer to internal power so that you can empower yourself to help with any living situation that you're dealing with. Of course, to understand this meditation practice, you need to understand the chakras or 'wheels' of the body. Your body contains these imaginary wheels, and they're supposedly lined in the center of your body. Each wheel is a chakra point, and it's not something that you can see. Chakra function is meant to regulate the functions of your body. Chakras are meant to rotate at a certain speed, but no matter what, it's supposed to regulate the part of the body that it's in. your first chakra is your root chakra, known as the Mula Chakra, and it governs the others. If you have a blockage in this chakra, it'll provide you too much stress. Base chakra will help you to handle your stress, but to do that it can't be blocked. It deals with you being grounded, and it even affects your sense of confidence.

Your second chakra is also known as the sacral chakra, and it is about an inch below your navel. It's related closely to the first chakra, but it has to deal with reproductive functions, and it will determine your sexual nature. If you have a blockage here, it'll affect your capacity to reproduce.

Next, you'll find your third chakra, which is also called your solar plexus. This is located right below the sternum. It determines both your power and your courage. This is considered to be a chakra that is powerful, and if you can fix a blockage here many people feel that you can turn your life around.

Your fourth chakra is also known as the heart chakra, and it's located next to your heart. It governs love life, but it also keeps track of the majority of your feelings. It's meant to work in tandem with your solar plexus chakra. If you have a blockage here, then you'll have a hard time getting in touch with your feelings or finding your true thoughts.

Your fifth chakra is in the center of your throat. That is why it is referred to as the throat chakra, and as its location might imply, it governs speech and communication. If you have a blockage with your fifth chakra, then you will have both a hard time communicating with others as well as a hard time listening to others.

Your sixth chakra is located between your eyebrows. It's commonly referred to as the third eye chakra for this reason, and it's supposed to help you with intuition. If you have a blockage here, you will often experience a hard time connecting spiritually. It's also hard to look towards your future when your third eye chakra is not functioning properly.

Your seventh chakra is at the crown of your head, and it's considered to be related to your mind. This chakra is supposed to directly relate to the dreams that you're having. If you have a blockage in this chakra, then it's likely you won't be able to improve your dreams. Now that you know the bases of chakra, then you'll be able to start by practicing kundalini meditation.

Steps:

1. You need to find a quiet corner, and then you'll need to imagine that there is a small ball of light that comes from within your base chakra, cleaning it from the inside out.

2. Start to imagine that it's starting to cleanse you of negative energy and is filling you up with positive energy.

3. Imagine that the energy is moving to the second chakra, drawing out the negativity energy from there as well. Continue to see this light going through each of your chakras, but don't force it to move too quickly.

4. When it's at the last chakra, imagine that it is piercing through that chakra and finally releasing the light.

This meditation is meant to chase away negative emotions as well as negative thoughts. It's supposed to force a sense of calm, helping to generate more positive dreams. You should do this at least once a week.

Qi Gong Meditation:

This is another wonderful meditation method that has a milder version of the pervious meditation. In this version, you don't have to visualize all of the chakras. It's simpler, and it helps when you're pinched on time.

Steps:

1. You need to start by sitting in a comfortable position, and you're going to need to be in a place that's quiet.

2. Start to visualize all of your chakras, and then think of it like a ball of water that's coming from your first one. It should cleanse like light would. This water should be spinning around, and you should move it up to your final chakra.

3. Imagine it going back down and back up again. You need to imagine that it's a loop that is cleansing your chakras as it moves up and down. Next, you're going to want to release it like you did the light.

Hypnosis Meditation:

This is another type of meditation that you can use to help cleanse your mind and control your dreams through positivity. Hypnosis is sending yourself into a trance on purpose, helping you to get closer to your subconscious mind. It's hard to induce hypnosis on yourself, so you may need someone else to help you meditate in this way. There are professional hypnotists that are able to help you, or you can teach yourself how to do it all on your own.

Steps:

1. Lay down in a comfortable position, and force your mind to be pushed back into itself.

2. Try to ask yourself what you might be holding in the back of your mind. Ask yourself if you're trying to hide anything from yourself.

3. Look at the images that come to mind, and let yourself sink deeper into your own mind. Let go the thoughts of your body, and only interact with the thoughts that appear. Look at anything that's troubling you.

4. Once you're done interacting with your subconscious, you'll want to snap your fingers so that you can come out of it.

Zazen:

This is a movement based meditation, and that movement helps you to focus and clear your thoughts, which will help you to clear your mind.

Steps:

1. Start by sitting in a comfortable position, and your eyes will need to be closed. Just make sure that you're choosing a position based solely on your comfort.

2. Rocking your body forward and then backward, and you need to make sure that the motion stays consistent. You should be able to zone in on the movement, making it easier to let go of anything that is boggling your mind down.

3. Just slow down and stop when you're ready to. Make sure that you give yourself five minutes to settle down and readjust.

Dreams & Positive Affirmation

You already know that meditation can help you with making your dreams positive. Negativity manifests in many ways in your life, and your dreams are one of them. Of course, you'll find that to promote positive dreams that you can decipher easily, positivity is needed. Of course, affirmations help you to guide your dreams as well. Positive affirmations are referring to positive thoughts that you believe, often repeating to yourself either out loud or in your head, and they're usually just a sentence that you decide on. In this chapter, you'll learn about some common positive affirmations that are used to control your dreams. You'll think that they're just sentences that are something you need to repeat, but they have more power than that so long as you believe in them.

My dreams will be positive.

This is one of the easiest affirmations to use, and you can swear by it. All you have to do is keep telling yourself that you will dream positively before bed. Positive dreaming is about getting into the right space, and this can help you to lucid dream as well because it'll help to make sure that you don't suffer from what your subconscious wants you to dream about, especially if it's negative. It is possible for you to control not only your dreams but also your dream patterns. All you have to do is keep telling yourself that you can, so keep that positivity in your thoughts with this positive affirmation.

I will lucid dream.

If you haven't mastered lucid dreaming already, this will help to make sure that you work towards lucid dreaming. If you do know how to lucid dream already, it will help you to lucid dream the night that you're thinking about it. Lucid dreaming will help to make sure that your dreams are positive because you'll be in control of them. Dreams can be considered a virtual reality, but you can turn them into a much more real reality with lucid dreaming. You don't want to say it just once, but you'll need to chant it repeatedly when you're trying to induce a lucid dream.

I won't allow for negativity.

You have to remind yourself that you can and will stave off the negativity in your life. By positively affirming that, then you'll be able to do this. It won't just make it disappear in your life, but it will make a large difference. All you need to do is continue to say it enough, and eventually you'll begin to unconsciously think it as well, helping to keep it away.

I will control my own dreams.

This is another way to make sure that you start lucid dreaming. You should also say this multiple times before bed, and you can say it upon waking to help as well. You don't want to just dream. You want to breathe life into them, and so you need to tell yourself that you can control every part of the dream from the landscape to the people that are in them. This is an affirmation that can also give you the ability to wake yourself up from a dream if you do experience a negative one. There is a difference between waking up from your dream because you're startled and waking up consciously so that you can go back to sleep and dream of something better. Waking yourself up on purpose is what should be aimed for.

I'll dream about what I desire.

This is another part of lucid dreaming, and if you're having a hard time dreaming about what you want, then this is the affirmation for you. It's a good thing to dream about what you actually want in life because it'll allow you to not only recognize your desires but also to reinforce them. By dreaming about positive achievements that you want, you have to explore how to get them in your dreams, giving you the fuel you need to reach them in the waking world.

Mindfulness & Your Dreams

You probably want only positive dreams, but this isn't possible. However, you can promote more positivity in your life which will create a more positive dream world on a regular basis. Dreaming positively can impact your life, and it can draw out the best in yourself. Bad dreams often stem from negative thoughts, bleeding into your waking world. It's something that you need to steer clear of. It can create a lot of positivity to when you're mindful.

Mindfulness is actually a concept that's existed for thousands of years, helping people to relax both their bodies and mind. There has been a lot of research done studying the effects of mindfulness on your mental state, and it's been proven to root out negative emotions and thoughts. It can instill you with positive feelings, and having a majority of positive feelings throughout your day will help to make your dreams much more positively. You should practice mindfulness on a day to day basis for the best results, but it can't be explained in just one sentence.

To remain mindful, then you need to pay attention to everything that's around you. Most people are constantly surrounded by one event after another with people talking all around them. It's a chaotic atmosphere, and it's hard to remain focused on anything besides the negative emotions and chaos. It's important to reel yourself in and try to be calm, and it can be hard to remain mindful of what's happening around you. You should always be fully aware of what you're doing, and the secret to being calm is to be alert. Don't allow yourself to lapse into a state of unconsciousness where your mind drifts. Many people travel to the back of their minds when engaging in their everyday life, and it only leads to unnecessary confusion and anxiety.

By learning mindfulness, you're learning how to cut the chaos out of your life in a healthy manner. Here is how to incorporate mindfulness in your everyday life.

- **It's a mental concept.** Mindfulness makes you pay attention to everything that's around you. You have to concentrate on activities, getting absorbed into them instead of absorbing into your own mind. Mindfulness will teach you how to focus on every task in front of you.

- **It acquaints you with your inner self.** Your dreams are a reflection of how you feel and think inside, and being mindful will help you to understand a little of what happens in your mind.

- **Events during the day do affect your feelings and thoughts.** The thoughts and feeling you have during the day will affect your dreams. Sometimes it will affect them more than others, so by being mindful and filling yourself up with positivity you can control your dreams to a much large extent.

- **Mindfulness should be a lifetime choice and not just a habit.** Mindfulness won't help that much unless you make it a lifestyle choice. Otherwise, negativity will just pile up and cause you too many issues to fix with a 'habit'. You will only benefit from mindfulness if you practice it on a day to day.

Next you'll learn about everyday exercises that you can use to improve your feelings and thoughts. Therefore, you'll be learning how to improve your dreams. Try to pick out the ones that you feel will make the largest impact in your life.

Mindfulness in Waking:

Waking up in the morning can set the atmosphere for your whole day. You don't want to have a cloudy thought process, so you should try to collect yourself as soon as you can after waking. So start by sitting on your bed for five minutes. Remain mindful that you're up now, and try to visualize the great day ahead of you. Don't be tempted to stay between the sheets and asleep for five more minutes, but you can still lay down for five minutes so long as you're mindful the entire time. Ask yourself how it feels to stay up, and it's best to get up and stretch so that you can are mindful of the limits of your body and how you feel in the morning.

Mindfulness in Brushing:

Brushing your teeth is usually what's next on your daily agenda, and you should be mindful about brushing your teeth. You shouldn't just rush to the bathroom. You should take up to five minutes to do a neat and mindful job. Pick up the brush, and be mindful about how much toothpaste you put on the brush, placing it on your teeth and slowly brushing. Be mindful of hitting each and every tooth, and close your eyes so that you can visualize the brush as it goes over each tooth. This will usually calm your body and mind. After you're done, then gently rinse your mouth and don't be in a hurry. There's no reason to move from one activity to another through rushing.

Mindfulness in Exercise:

Exercising every morning is a great addition to your routine, and by tiring out your body throughout the day, you're likely to dream better as well. However, you will want to perform mindfulness exercises if you want to get the most out of your dreams later. Picking something like jogging is usually best. It's something that you can keep in mind how your body feels when you're jogging, and you should absorb yourself in your activity. Don't allow yourself to be distracted by what's going on around you. After you're done, take a moment to cool down and be mindful of your heartbeat and breathing before you head back home.

Mindfulness in Bathing:

Indulging in mindful bathing or even taking a shower is an experience that's therapeutic, and many people do it before bed. It can leave you with a feeling of being refreshed, but you should take your shower or bath leisurely. Remember not to rush through or that's not being mindful. Concentrate on how it feels to have the soap run over your skin and what your soap smells like. You should remain in the shower or bath for about thirty minutes, taking everything slow and trying to clean your mind as well as your body. You increase your chances of good dreams from this exercise by doing it an hour or two before bed.

Mindfulness in Cooking & Eating:

When you're cooking, it's easy to become distracted. By being mindful of cooking, you can use it as a stress reliever so that the stress doesn't bleed over into your dreams. Spend time to enjoy the act of cooking, and remain mindful of what you're doing. Don't let you prepare your meal half-hearted, and make sure that you can zone in. you can also being mindful in eating by making sure that you're sitting down at the table and taking your time. This can be hard to do when you're eating with your family, but you should remain focused on your meal. Make sure to cut your food in small pieces so that you can savor it, exploring it leisurely. Don't hurry, and it's even more helpful when you close your eyes to savor the bite.

Mindfulness in Meditation:

Mindfulness in meditation before bed or during the day when you're stressed is a great way to make sure that any other emotions you're having is cleared before bed. Concentrate on your inner self when you're meditating. Make sure to observe your feelings, thoughts and emotions, and you shouldn't interact with them. Be mindful of your body when you're meditating as well, concentrating on your heartbeat and your breathing as well as how it affects your body.

Mindfulness in Sleep:

This mindfulness practice more directly affects your dreams. Prepare yourself to sleep peacefully, so don't just head to bed and try to sleep peacefully. Be mindful of how your body starts to relax as you go to sleep, taking deep and even breathes. By tensing and relaxing your body, being aware of how you feel during it, you're more likely to relax and even remember your dreams.

Dream Tips & Reminders

Here are a few things that you need to remember when you're dealing with dreams, and you'll even find some tips in this chapter that will help you to interpret and deal with your dreams. These tips will help you to make it easier to lucid dream as well, but there are many things that you'll need to avoid and pay attention to. Keep in mind that your subconscious creates your dreams, even if we aren't completely sure why dreams occur, and so you do have a part in making them even if you aren't a lucid dreamer yet.

Symbols Often Aren't Direct

In your dreams there are always symbols, but symbols are not always obvious. Sometimes, symbols are something in the background and not the forefront, and sometimes they are personal and not universal. The symbols you find in your dream are coded by your subconscious to try to tell your conscious mind something in the only way it knows how. Many people make the mistake that believing that symbols are direct. If you're dreaming about killing your brother and then running away, this doesn't mean that you secretly want to kill your brother. It just could mean that you feel guilty over a fight that you had. Symbols are there to symbolize something, and it's not always obvious. Always keep your mind open to the different possibilities.

Remember What Happened:

You should remember what happened right before you went to sleep because this could be the code you need to decipher your dreams. You'll likely dream about what's on your mind or pressing to the situation right before you lay down. If you fought with someone before sleep, then that is likely the reason you're fighting with someone in the dream. Just keep in mind that your dreams are a reflection of your inner mind, and so anything that is on your mind is likely to manifest in the dream world. Paying attention to the waking world, your feelings on these situations, and issues you may be having, is the best way to decode the dreams that you're dealing with.

Only the Past & Present:

Keep in mind that dreams cannot tell you the future. They can show you your past, and they can show you how you're feeling in the present. However, many people fear that they are seeing the future. If you do see something that is a possible future, then you need to remember that this isn't a sure thing. This is just something that your mind feels is a possible future. You can change it, and it often just reflects your own fears.

Fears Can Be Overcome:

Nightmares are often a result of fear, and it is important to remember that everyone suffers through fear. The worst thing that you can do for yourself is to believe that there is nothing you can do but to be afraid, especially when it comes to your dreams. Just because you're having nightmares on a regular basis doesn't mean that you won't be able to overcome these fears eventually. Facing your fears by learning lucid dreaming is usually the best way to face these fears. Try the visualization method if you want to overcome these fears, and trying to think of a different outcome where your fear doesn't win is a great way to get rid of them almost entirely. Of course, some fears will only lessen, but trying to overcome your fears is the best course of action.

Lucid Dreaming Takes Time:

You need to keep in mind that lucid dreaming is a skill. Just like any other skill, it can take time to master it. You need to be patient, so you'll need to keep working at it even if you fail on multiple occasions. It's also important to remember that there is more than one method out there. There are even more tips and tricks that you can use for learning lucid dreaming a well. Some people will pick up lucid dreaming after just a few times, but others will take many different methods and many different days before they find a way to lucid dream. Even if you do end up lucidly dreaming once, it doesn't mean that you'll be able to do it whenever you want just yet.

Don't Eat Too Much:

Make sure that you don't eat a large meal before bed. Digestion is a lot of work for your body, and you'll find that it can actually disrupt sleep cycles as well. It's best not to eat heavy foods or fatty foods before you actually go to sleep. It's best not to eat within two hours of trying to rest, and you should beware of spicy or acidic foods as well. Spicy and acidic foods can cause heartburn as well as indigestion. If you do have to eat before bed, try to eat something that is light and healthy. Some crackers, a piece of fruit, or even a slice of toast is recommended if you can't avoid eating.

Avoid Alcohol:

It's best to avoid alcohol before bed as this will also disrupt your sleep cycle. Many people prefer a nightcap before bed, but this isn't wise if you are suffering from nightmares. You also shouldn't have alcohol before bed if you are trying to practice lucid dreaming. Just like with food, try not to have alcohol two hours before you go to bed. All alcohol should be avoided before bed, not just liquor. Alcohol may be good during the day, but it can be one of the worst things for you if you're trying to dream peacefully or practice lucid dreaming.

Don't Sleep Stressed:

You should never sleep stressed out because this is going to ensure that you don't sleep well most of the time. It can disrupt your ability to cause a lucid dream, and it can even cause nightmares. It can also cause you to have more symbols and messages in your dreams, and your stress can complicate these symbols, making it even harder to interpret what your subconscious is trying to tell you. Try to do something that will help you to unwind before you sleep. Thirty minutes is the minimum time that you should use, but you'll find that it's best to wind down for an hour or more. many people will read before bed, but if you don't like reading, try to find something that you do enjoy doing that isn't going to keep you up or stress you out.

A Guide to Settling in to Dream

It's easier said than done to have pleasant dreams, especially if you want them to be easy to remember and interpret. However, there is a way to sleep tight and have the sweet dreams that you crave. It's important to have your body have a rest, and therefore REM has to be possible. You only experience REM for roughly 90 to 120 minutes per night, and it's a short time compared to the time you are fully asleep. However, that means you are able to have six to seven intense dreams in one night, so it's important you use this chapter to learn how to fall asleep the right way to create the right dreaming atmosphere. This will give you a chance to interpret your dreams for hidden memories and connections because you'll get a better night's sleep. It can even help you to wake up in the morning feeling more energized and ready to take on the day ahead.

Step 1: Create a Bedtime Routine

Create a routine if you want to ensure a good night's rest. Carrying a routine every night before you to go bed will start to cue your body and mind into the fact that it needs to tart shutting down because rest will be soon. This routine can include taking a long bath or hot shower before bed, relaxing on the couch, reading a few chapters of a book, listening to music, or anything that you feel will help you to relax. Of course, keep in mind that it's best to avoid electronic devices such as mobile phones, TVs, tablets, or any other device before bed since hat type of light will often lead to a disrupted sleep pattern.

Step 2: Ensuring Your Comfort

You have to be comfortable if you want to get a good night's rest. That means you have to have a comfortable environment. Most people don't pay attention to their environment, but your body picks up on the environment you're in even when you're asleep. A cool, quiet and dark room is always best. If you live in a noisy neighborhood for example, then you may want to invest in something like ear plugs to block out that sound. If your area is tow arm, then an air condition or fan will help you to sleep better. If you can't get your room dark enough, investing in darkening drapes or a sleep mask will help you to sleep easier as well. Your bedding will also play a role in how well you sleep, so it's important to have a comfortable pillow and bed.

Step 3: Make Sure to Regulate Naps

Naps during the day often seem like a good idea, but they can damage your nighttime routine. Therefore, you need to actually limit how long your naps are during the day. If you do take a nap, try to keep it at about a half hour. You should only take it during mid-afternoon. Your room should be dark enough or that you at least have a sleep mask on no matter when you sleep. Your natural clock can be disrupted when you're sleeping during hours where sunlight starts to seep into the room.

Step 4: Always Relax Before Sleeping

Go to sleep each and every night relaxed, and your head should be clear of anything that's bothering you or your dreams will be negatively affected. You shouldn't be thinking of too much or doing too much before bed because it's your sleep and dreams that will suffer. Consider stress management techniques. Even a cup of tea before bed and a few minutes to yourself can go a long ways. Make sure to organize and delegate duties if you can, and make sure that you take a break from anything that's bothering you. Learn to save it for tomorrow so that you don't stress out.

Step 5: Make an Exercise Routine

Your sleep will get much better if you're exercising daily. It's been proven that if you exercise regularly, then you'll sleep better. You're also much less likely to want to sleep during the day, and exercise can help with insomnia as well as sleep apnea. It can also increase how much time you actually spend in REM, which can make it easier for you to remember your dreams. However, you may not realize until you've been at it for a few months. Still, you do need to be careful about when you exercise so that you don't negatively affect your dreams. Exercising can increase your metabolism, temperature and it can stimulate the release of hormones in your body. If you are exercising during the day, then it won't hurt your sleep and dreams. However, if you do so before you sleep, then it will interfere with your dreams. Any heavy workout shouldn't be done within three hours before sleep. Keep in mind that some people take longer to cool down than others. Some people can actually take around six hours to cool down, so keep the exercise early in your day.

Some More Dream Symbols

To understand your dreams, especially when lucid dreaming, you're going to want to learn a little more about dream symbols. Of course, you'll find that there are many dream symbols out there, and this book can only cover some of the more common ones.

Crocodile, Alligator, or Large Reptile:

If you're dreaming of a large reptile, usually an alligator or crocodile, then you need to watch out for a potential attack. It could be an end to your career or place in an organization. This attack is usually a verbal one because they have large mouths, and they're known for their dangerous bite. This is something that your subconscious knows and is trying to use to help to warn you against it. Their intent is to take you down completely, and so these words can damage your reputation and turn people against you. These creatures often lie low, making them hard to see, so you need to be careful of those around you.

Even the ones you're having a hard time noticing. If you die in your dreams because of this reptile, then it can represent a fear of losing a position that you have in life. If it just bites you but you survive, then it's trying to tell you that you don't think that the attack will be deadly. Of course, that doesn't mean the bite will be painless. It'll take a while for you to heal. The other alternative is that the creature tries to chase you, but this doesn't mean that they catch you, and it can be trying to warn you that you're provoking someone or you're messing with something that could come back to bite you.

Houses:

Houses are usually something personal in your life, and it doesn't mean you're dreaming about the house that you actually have. You may be dreaming about your dream home or just somewhere that feels like home. The condition of the home you're in means a lot, and if it's in good condition then your inner sanctuary is in good condition. Of course, that doesn't mean that a cave home can't be in good condition. It can just mean that you're hiding your inner self. If you feel cramped, that's when you know that you are under stress.

If it needs repairing, you'll show that there is something of yourself that you'll need to address such as health issues. The owner of the house that you're in also matters because you may not always be dreaming about a house that you own. If it's a house that you grew up in, then what you're trying to tell yourself usually has to do with your past, especially your childhood. If it's anyone else's house then it is probably that you're playing an important role in someone else's life or they're playing a big one in yours. You still need to pay attention to the exact room you're in as well. It can show you what your mind is trying to tell you by knowing what type of issue you're having. The bedroom is usually because you need to rest or it's dealing with something that's intimate.

If it's an attic, it's probably because it's pointing to something you've forgotten or at least tried to forget. It can show that you need to dredge up the past to solve the issues that are at hand. A family room shows that action requiring communication needed to be taken. Bathrooms are often a place of cleansing, as we've covered as well, but it could show that you need to cross personal space or boundaries as well. If you're dreaming about the kitchen, it can show that you need food spiritually or that you're trying to prepare for something in your life.

Aircraft Dreams:

It specifically says 'aircraft' because in your dreams it isn't always practical. You may be dreaming of an airplane, a helicopter or even a boat in the sky. Who knows, you might even be dreaming about a steampunk blimp, but it'll still have the same meaning. If you're dreaming of being in an aircraft, it's usually referring back to a hospital, corporation, a hospital or something that you belong to because it refers to something bigger than yourself. Of course, if you're looking to see what group it belongs to, then you can always look at the clues that are onboard, including the people that are on the aircraft with you.

The size of the aircraft also matters because larger aircrafts usually show that the company has bigger influences. If it's a helicopter, you probably aren't dreaming about something that's influenced a lot by others. You may be trying to save someone in your life. If you're on a private jet, then it's representing a personal mission that you need to go on. However, if it crashes, then it's because it splits into a disaster, usually a personal one such as having to leave the people that it represents behind. If people survive the crash, then it's showing you the people you still want to keep close even if you're trying to separate yourself from the whole.

Automobile:

Once again, you'll find that we're using the term automobile because there are different types. Your car usually is a representation of what is driving you. What you drive in your dream doesn't always show what you actually drive. Of course, try to pay attention to what your automobile looks like. You should pay attention to the size, name, style, color and anything at all that stands out. The way you're approaching what drives you such as your attitude. If you have a large king ring for example, then it shows that there are often multiple steps. If you're driving a truck, it shows that you're willing to care a heavy load or burden. If you're dreaming of an animated vehicle, then it shows that you work with children or that you need to handle things as you would handle things with a child.

If it's red, then you're probably because you're looking for recklessness and you may be experiencing anger. If you've lost that car, then it shows that you're having a hard time focusing. If you're driving a convertible, then you're probably open to positivity. If it's during the rain or something makes you feel negative about it, then it's saying you need to protect yourself. If you have a large vehicle, then it shows that you have a large drive or capacity to reach your goals. If the car is in bad condition, then it can show that you are neglecting yourself and what matters to you.

If you're in the wrong lane, then it can show that you aren't doing what you are supposed to be doing. At least, it shows that you don't feel like you are. If you're going in reverse, then it can show that you're approaching a situation in the wrong way. If the car is out of control, it can show that you don't have faith in yourself or your ability to lead your own life. If you are in a car accident, then it shows that there is a clash of goals or ideas in your life. If your car is flying, then it shows that you believe you need to rise above your circumstances. If you are moving the car with your feet, then it shows that you feel you're out of gas and need to find a way to keep from feeling drained.

Boats:

If the boat is small, it shows that there is a small influence. The larger the boat will usually signify the larger the influence. A ship is meant to carry different people over a larger distance, and it's usually mission minded. Of course, some can be for more fun reasons. You need to look at the type of boat that you're on, such as if you feel you're on a cruise ship, a ship that seems to be an older one like a pirate ship, or a small cabin that's mission minded. For example, if you're on a sailboat, then it may represent a church because it's moved by the wind, but it usually has a spiritual meaning.

If you're on a boat that is carrying others, for example a tug boat, then you're probably telling yourself that you're supporting a lot of people. A speed boat is telling you that you need to look for something in your life that is exciting and may pass you up to quickly. Your subconscious probably doesn't want you to miss this opportunity unless you feel as if you're running away from something. Then it's usually because you feel you're in danger.

If you're having to row your own boat, then it shows that you're putting in a lot of effort into something, usually it means that you feel you either need to put in more or if you're feeling overwhelmed your mind is trying to remind you of how taxing what you're doing is. If you're on a fishing boat, then it usually shows that you feel stranded and are still hoping for something, looking for something. Remember that boats are a journey. It shows that you're in a transition.

Bathroom:

The bathroom is meant to clean out toxins in your body, so if you're having dreams about the bathroom, then you know you need to cleanse yourself. This could be religious or something that you're doing needs to stop. If you're in a public place and having a bathroom dream, then you know that you can't keep this cleanse a secret. If you're having a shower dream, then you're cleansing yourself from outer toxins such as the exposure you have to other people in your life or your environment as a whole.

If you're washing or even conditioning your hair, then you know that it most likely has to do with cleansing your mind. If you're in a bathtub, often soaking, then you're liking trying to tell yourself that you need a spiritual cleanse. If you are dreaming about the actual toilet, then it's usually a deeper cleanse of toxins that are inside of you such as your emotions. It can also show that you're under a lot of pressure. If you are trying to find a toilet but can't, then it can show that you can't find a way to cleanse yourself but you're still recognizing that you need to. If you're grooming yourself, usually in front of a mirror, it shows that you think you need to polish up your act and prepare for something.

Dreams of Reckless Behavior:

If you're dreaming about reckless behavior then your subconscious is often trying to tell you that you're making poor behavioral decisions. It can be your mind trying to tell you that you lose control of yourself too often. Dreams of reckless behavior can be a form of wake up call, and it's your brain telling you that you shouldn't act out. Your subconscious is well aware of what you're trying not to admit to and the penalties that can happen because of it.

Storms:

Storms in your dreams may seem pretty obvious that there is a storm in your life. It can be something that's atmospheric, such as emotional, financial, physical, emotional or spiritual. Winds of change can be both good and bad, but a storm will always show that there are changes in your life. If it's oncoming, it can easily represent dark times that are coming, but you need to keep in mind that all storms do pass. If the storm isn't too dark, such as if it's just windy or light colored, then it can be that there is an uncomfortable time that you're experiencing but still change will come. However, you feel like there will be a positive outcome if you are seeing this type of storm. The darker the storm, the more destructive you feel it will be, and often it means you feel like the aftermath will be destructive as well.

Dogs/Canines:

Dogs aren't considered to be a favorable sign in your dreams unless it's a dog that you grew up with, took care of and loved. However, they can be if the feelings are there. Analyze your feelings towards the dog. If they're friendly, then it may be a best friend, a family member, or someone who's passed away. Of course, if you feel negatively in this dream, then it most likely is that something is vicious and able to attack you.

Dogs can symbolize different things because they're both wild animals sometimes but often considered to be a loyal animal and a people pleaser. If you're dreaming about a dog that it supposed to help you, such as a seeing-eye dog, then it could show that you depend on someone or that someone is depending on you but you feel like you're stumbling along.

If you're dreaming of a hound dog, then it may be that you're protecting someone. If it's a dog that's often a police dog, then it shows that something needs to be checked in a legal way. A retriever will show you that you feel you've lost something, and it may be something spiritual or emotional which isn't always obvious. If you're dreaming about a bulldog, it may be that you're feeling stubborn or that someone you're trying to calm down is too stubborn.

If you're dreaming of puppies, then it could easily show that you are thinking of children or want a child. However, if it's a bad dream about puppies, it could show that you're feeling like you're in a relationship with someone that is too immature. Dreaming about a pack of dogs is common as well, and if they're biting you or even chasing you, then it means that the people that you care about may be turning on you.

If it's just growling or trying to bite you, especially if it's behind you, then it may be that they're hiding it a little easier. If someone is hurting a dog you care about, then it's showing that you feel people that you care about may be trying to hurt those close to you. If it's someone else's dog or property, then it shows that you've crossed a line with someone and you know it.

Some Dream Trivia

If you want to understand your dreams, then this chapter on dream trivia should help to shed just a little more light on how you dream. Your dream world is interesting, and these facts should help to enhance your insight on the subject.

Most of Your Dreams You Won't Remember:

You'll likely not remember 90% of your dreams, and you'll have to work on remembering more of your dreams. It can be a skill, and you can remember more if you train yourself but you can only do this for the REM portion of your sleep. Your REM phase will only last for about ten minutes, and, and since you go through more than one REM cycle, so you'll have more than one dream cycle to continue. Just remember that in dreams time doesn't work the same, so even if you're only dreaming about it for a few minutes, it can seem like your dream lasted hours or days.

Women Often Experience More Nightmares:

Women are known to dream more about their family, children and other household matters. This is a stressor to them, and it can cause women to have more nightmares than others. This is why it's important for women to try to distance themselves from all problems before they go to bed. It can be hard for women to remember that their family issues are also something that they need to let go of at least temporarily before they go to bed.

You Only See Faces You Know:

You actually only dream of people that you know because it isn't possible for your minds to generate a face that you haven't seen. If you think you've seen a stranger in your dream, you've probably seen them somewhere. You probably forgot about them consciously, but that doesn't mean your subconscious mind has forgotten them. Usually the people that you've seen in your life will appear in one of your dreams at least once. Of course, your conscious mind isn't aware of everything that your unconscious mind picks up. Your brain is always collecting data such as impressions, people, shapes, feelings, and a large variety of other factors that will always go into some part of your memory. You just can't access most of these memories, but that information commonly spills out into your dreams.

Not Everyone Dreams in Color:

You'll find that twelve percent of people who can remember their dreams actually only dream in black and white. It doesn't have anything to do with their eye sight because they can usually see color in their day to day life. Blind people dream vividly as well. Even those that have been blind since birth can dream, but most of their dreams are auditory, so their other senses can be stimulated as well such as smell, touch and even taste.

Most Emotions are Negative When Sleeping:

Most of the emotions that people experience in their dreams are negative, and you'll often feel anxious when dreaming instead of calm and relaxed. The non-rational nature of a dream can keep you remaining anxious throughout the entire dream, and it supports the theory that dreams are meant to let you come to terms with the feelings that bother you in the waking world. Most negative feelings of fear, anxiety and guilt come out in dreams because we repress them in the waking world.

Babies Don't Dream About Themselves:

For some reason, babies can't dream about themselves until they're five. However, this doesn't mean that babies don't have dreams. They do, but they usually just dream about random images and sounds. Many people believe that it's because they don't have an understanding of themselves until they're five.

Men & Women Don't Dream the Same:

Research has found that men usually dream of other men more often. About seventy percent of people that they see in their dreams are other men. On the other hand, women dream of an equal number of men and women. Men are also known to experience more heightened emotions when they dream, and women don't experience emotions in their dream well. It's possible that it has to deal with men usually repressing their feelings more. Women as well as men are equally emotional people, but social norms tell men that they shouldn't express those feelings. This is one reason that many people believe emotions come out for men in their dreams more.

Precognitive Dreams are Actually Common:

Many dreams can tell you about an event that's upcoming in your life. Many people call this déjà vu because you've seen an upcoming event. These are often experienced in everyday situations, and it's not out of the ordinary. It's either completely accidental or it's a prediction that your unconscious mind has made based on the circumstances you've experienced and the data that your subconscious has collected. However, your conscious thought process hasn't been able to realize that yet.

Many Adults Orgasm in Their Dreams:

This is mainly in males, and it's called a wet dream. Of course, it usually happens during a sexually themed dream, and it's a common phenomenon, especially when males reach puberty. Of course, that doesn't mean that women can't experience these dreams as well. There's no reason to feel embarrassed, and it doesn't matter how old the person is.

You Cannot Read or Tell Time If You're Sleep Walking:

If you're sleepwalking, you actually can't perform these two tasks. Sleepwalking affects many people, and you can do a variety of things when you're sleeping, including dangerous things. It's when your system fails to keep you from moving during a dream, which leads you to act out the dream in real life. If a dream involves a dreamer jumping through a window, for example, then the dreamer will do something similar. However, what a sleepwalker can't do is read something or tell the time.

Sleep Paralysis Keeps You Asleep When Dreaming:

Sleep paralysis keeps you asleep during a dream because you become partially paralyzed, making you unable to move. However, if you're sleepwalking that's because this doesn't occur. Lucid dreams will begin to live it out, but sleep paralysis will keep you from acting out the dream and doing anything dangerous in real life. Moving is able to wake you up, which is one reason sleep paralysis occurs.

People Can Actually Daydream:

There are some people that are able to dream while they're awake, and it's the opposite of sleepwalking. Your body is awake, but your mind drifts off into a state that's extremely similar to what happens when you dream. This is called a daydream, and it can result in an actual dream which leaves an individual confused on what is and isn't real.

Conclusion

Now that you know about dream interpretation and lucid dreaming, the last thing to do is try it yourself. Remember to write down your dreams, and above all, remember that you won't get everything down pact the moment you start trying. Both dream interpretation and learning lucid dreaming takes time. Both have several benefits and all you need is a little practice and patience. You already know the steps; you just need to put it into practice.

Good Luck!

And lastly, can I ask you for a small favor?

If you liked this book, can you please rate it on Amazon.

Please go to amazon.com to post your thoughts.

Your rating and review will really help me.

Thank you so much!

In case you are interested, here are some of the other best-selling books from my Publisher.

BRAIN: 51 Powerful Ways to Improve Brain Power, Enhance Memory, Intelligence and Concentration NATURALLY!

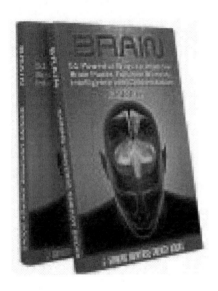

Please get your copy here http://lrd.to/brain

Depression: 101 Powerful Ways to Beat Depression, Stress, Anxiety and Be Happy NATURALLY!

This book is not just for people suffering from depression but for everyone who want to lead a happy and fulfilled life.

Please go to this link to get a copy

http://lrd.to/depression

Thank you and happy reading!

Printed in Poland
by Amazon Fulfillment
Poland Sp. z o.o., Wrocław